People I am Thankful for

Name	What they mean to me

Things I am Grateful for

1.
2.
3.
4.
5.
6.
7.
8.
9.
10.
11.
12.
13.
14.
15.
16.
17.
18.
19.
20.

Daily Gratitude

1.
2.
3.
4.
5.
6.
7.
8.
9.
10.
11.
12.
13.
14.
15.
16.
17.
18.
19.
20.
21.
22.
23.
24.
25.
26.
27.
28.
29.
30.
31.

Daily Gratitude

1.
2.
3.
4.
5.
6.
7.
8.
9.
10.
11.
12.
13.
14.
15.
16.
17.
18.
19.
20.
21.
22.
23.
24.
25.
26.
27.
28.
29.
30.
31.

Favorite Fall and Thanksgiving Quotes

There is always, always something to be thankful for.

Autumn is a second Spring when every leaf is a flower.
- Albert Camus

Be thankful for everything every single day.

Fall is sweater weather, crunchy leaves and pumpkin spice.

Be thankful for what you have; you'll end up having more.
- Oprah Winfrey

Gratitude turns what we have into enough.
- Melody Beattie

Favorite Fall and Thanksgiving Quotes

Favorite Fall and Thanksgiving Quotes

Thanksgiving Planning Calendar

October

MON	TUES	WED	THURS	FRI	SAT	SUN
☐	☐	☐	☐	☐	☐	☐
☐	☐	☐	☐	☐	☐	☐
☐	☐	☐	☐	☐	☐	☐
☐	☐	☐	☐	☐	☐	☐
☐	☐	☐	☐	☐	☐	☐

NOTES

Thanksgiving Planning Calendar

November

MON	TUES	WED	THURS	FRI	SAT	SUN
☐	☐	☐	☐	☐	☐	☐
☐	☐	☐	☐	☐	☐	☐
☐	☐	☐	☐	☐	☐	☐
☐	☐	☐	☐	☐	☐	☐
☐	☐	☐	☐	☐	☐	☐

NOTES

_____

_____

_____

_____

Weekly Planner

Monday

Tuesday

Wednesday

Thursday

Tasks

Week of

Shopping List

Friday

Saturday

Sunday

Notes

Budget

Month

Item	Budget	Actual
Regular Monthly Expenses		
Food		
Refreshments		
Décor		
Table Decor		
Outings		
Thanksgiving Cards		
Thanksgiving DIY Gifts and Crafts		
Entertainment		

Fall Weekly Exercise Plan

	Warm Up	Workout	Duration	Notes
Mon				
Tues				
Wed				
Thurs				
Fri				
Sat				
Sun				

Weekly Yard Work Schedule

	Task	How Often	Person Responsible	Notes
Mon				
Tues				
Wed				
Thurs				
Fri				
Sat				
Sun				

Fall Activity Ideas

Activity	Adults	Kids	All Ages	Notes

Places to Visit During Fall

Place	Cost	Notes

Color-Fall Scenic Trips

Destination	Route	Walk	Cycle	Car	Train	Notes

Planning Notes

Recipe Index

Recipe	Source	Make Ahead

Recipe for

Ingredients | **Method**

Cooking and Baking Notes

Our Thanksgiving Traditions

Tradition	Who started it
	When it began

Tradition	Who started it
	When it began

Tradition	Who started it
	When it began

Creating New Traditions

For the Adults

For the Children

Thanksgiving Decorations

Decorations Inventory	✓

Decorations Shopping List	✓

Thanksgiving Decorations Plan

- Outside
- Door & Entrance
- Living Room
- Stairs
- Bathrooms
- Kitchen
- Dining Room
- Thanksgiving Table

Thanksgiving Dinner – Dining Out

Host:	
Venue:	
Time:	
RSVP'd	

To Take

Menu

Preparations	✓
Gifts for hosts	
Drinks	
Thanksgiving Dinner Contributions	

Thanksgiving Invitation List

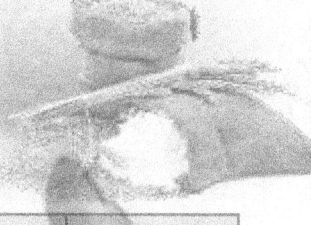

Name	Address	Sent	RSVP'd

Thanksgiving Guest List

Total Guests

Name	RSVP'd	Special Requests	Bringing

Thanksgiving Dinner

Menu

- Starter
- Main
- Dessert
- Snacks and Drinks

Family & Guests at the Table	Adults	Children

Thanksgiving Menu

	Who's Bringing	To Buy	✓
STARTERS			
TURKEY			
SIDES			
DESSERT			
DRINKS			

Thanksgiving Shopping List

Dairy	✓

Produce	✓

Meat	✓

Canned	✓

Baking	✓

Other	✓

Thanksgiving Wednesday Prep

To Do	✓

To Cook	✓

Notes

Thanksgiving Dinner Cooking Schedule

Date

Time		To Do	✓
5:00 AM			
6:00 AM			
7:00 AM			
8:00 AM			
9:00 AM			
10:00 AM			
11:00 AM			
12:00 PM			
1:00 PM			
2:00 PM			
3:00 PM			
4:00 PM			
5:00 PM			
6:00 PM			
7:00 PM			
8:00 PM			
9:00 PM			

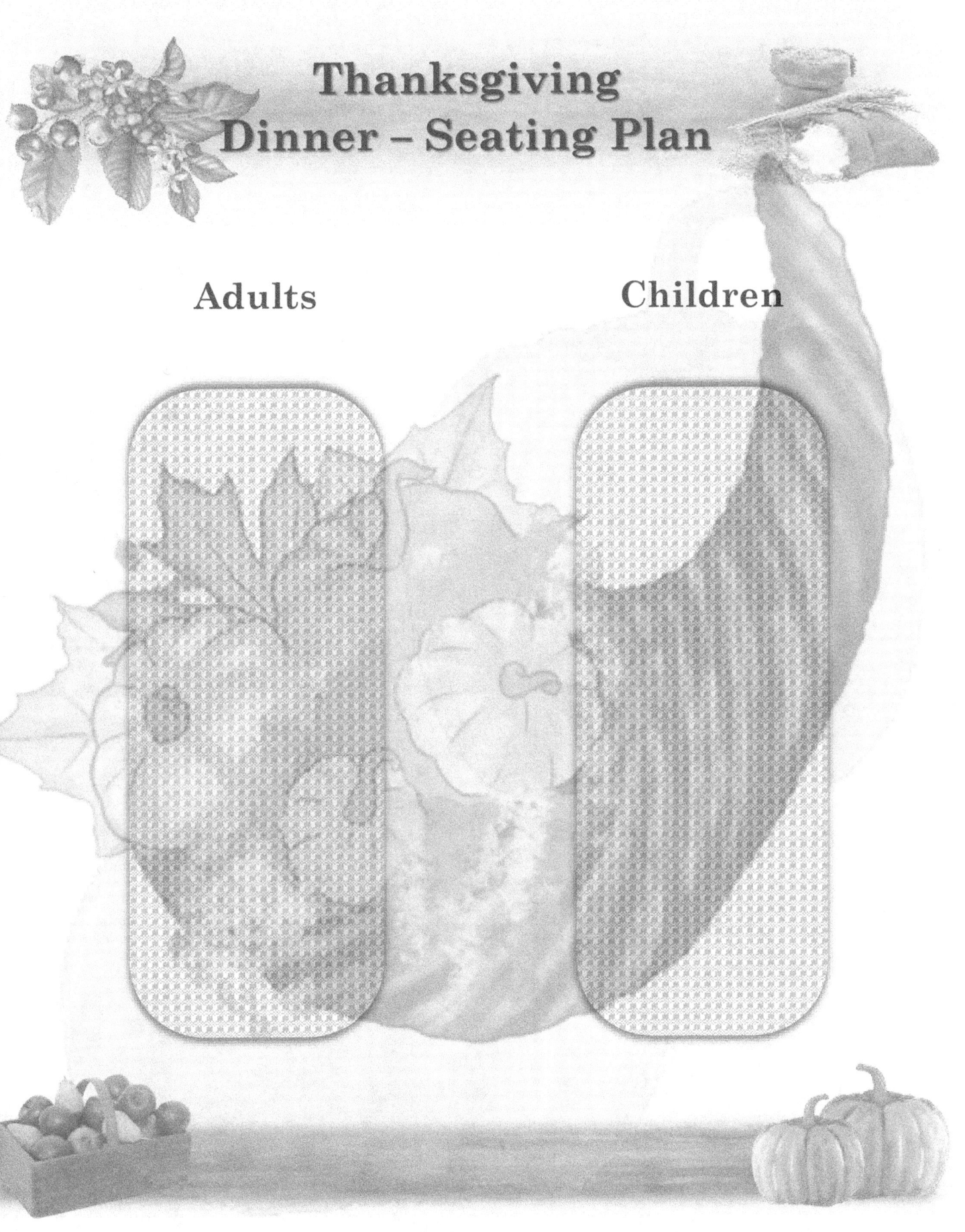

Thanksgiving Dinner

Seating Plan

Gifts Received

Name	Gift	"Thank you" sent

Using Leftovers

Idea	Recipe Source	Notes

Black Friday Wish List

Item	Where Available	Cost

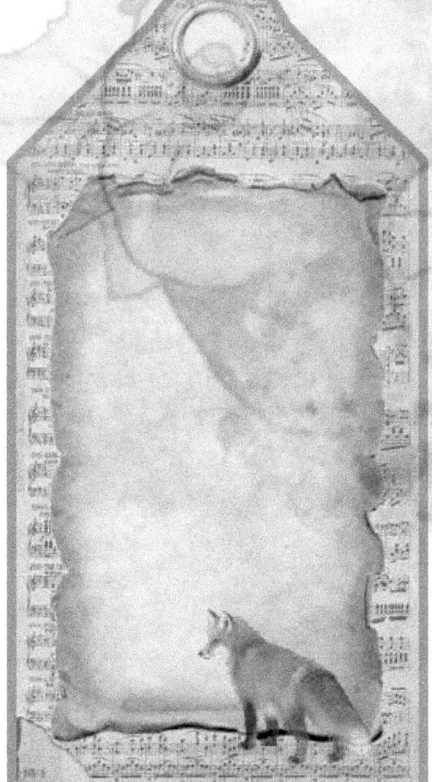
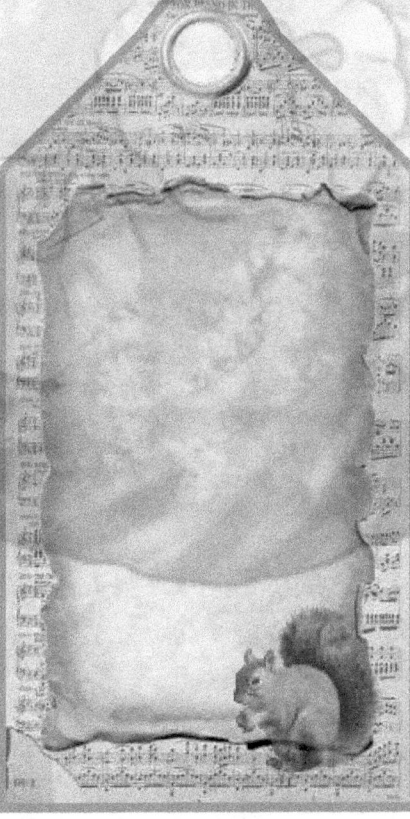
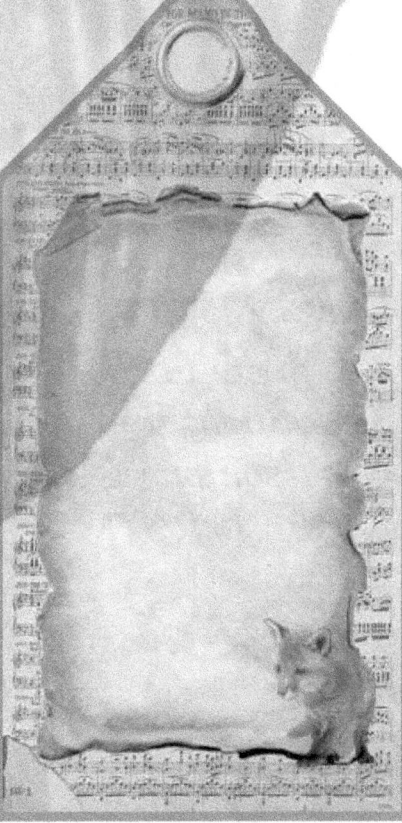

Conversation Starters

What is your Favorite Thanksgiving Food?

I am thankful for...

My favorite thing about Thanksgiving is...

What are you grateful for about the person on your Left?

The Thanksgiving tradition I enjoy the most is...

My favorite Thanksgiving family tradition is...

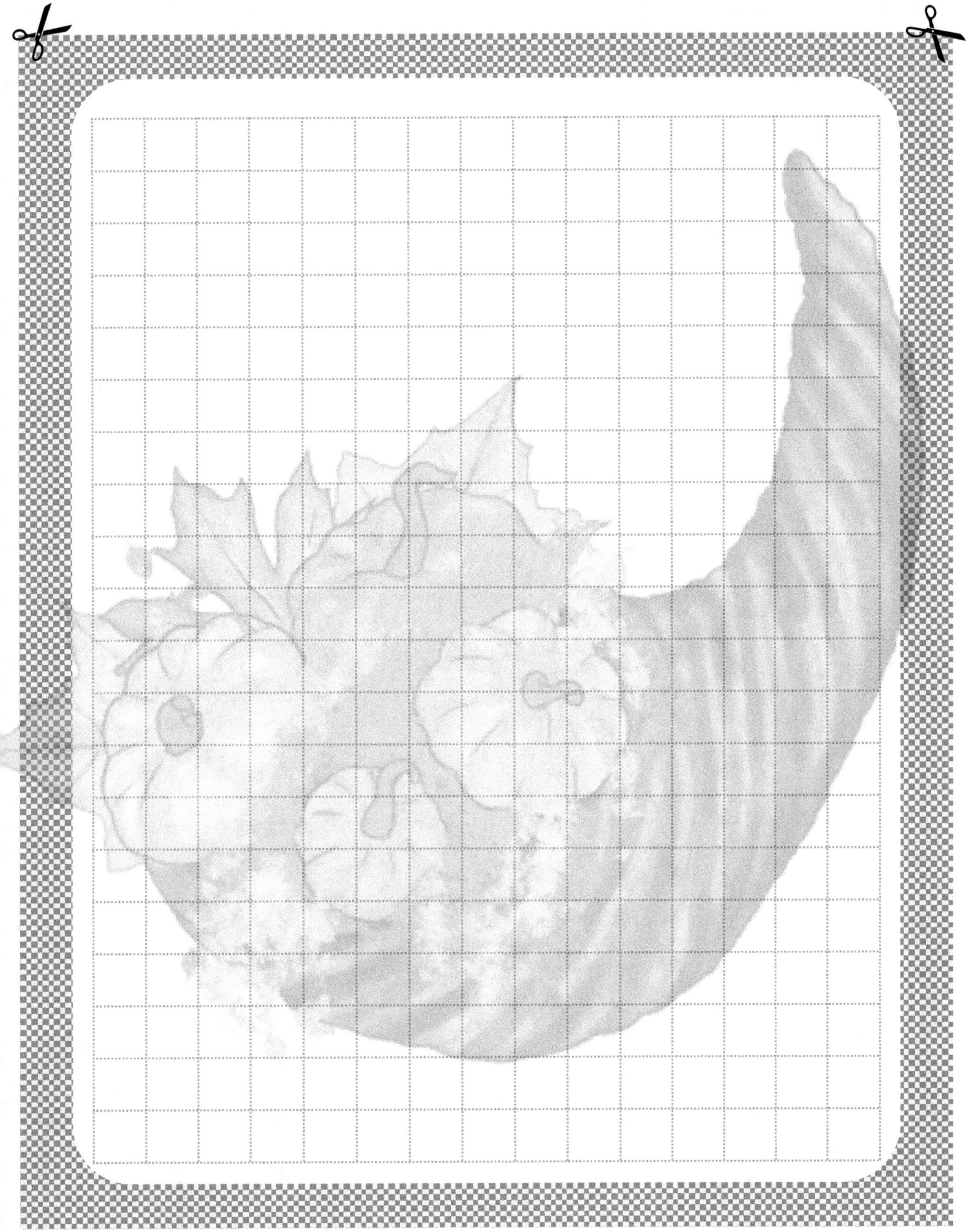

Count Your Blessings

1 2 3 4 5
6 7 8 9 10

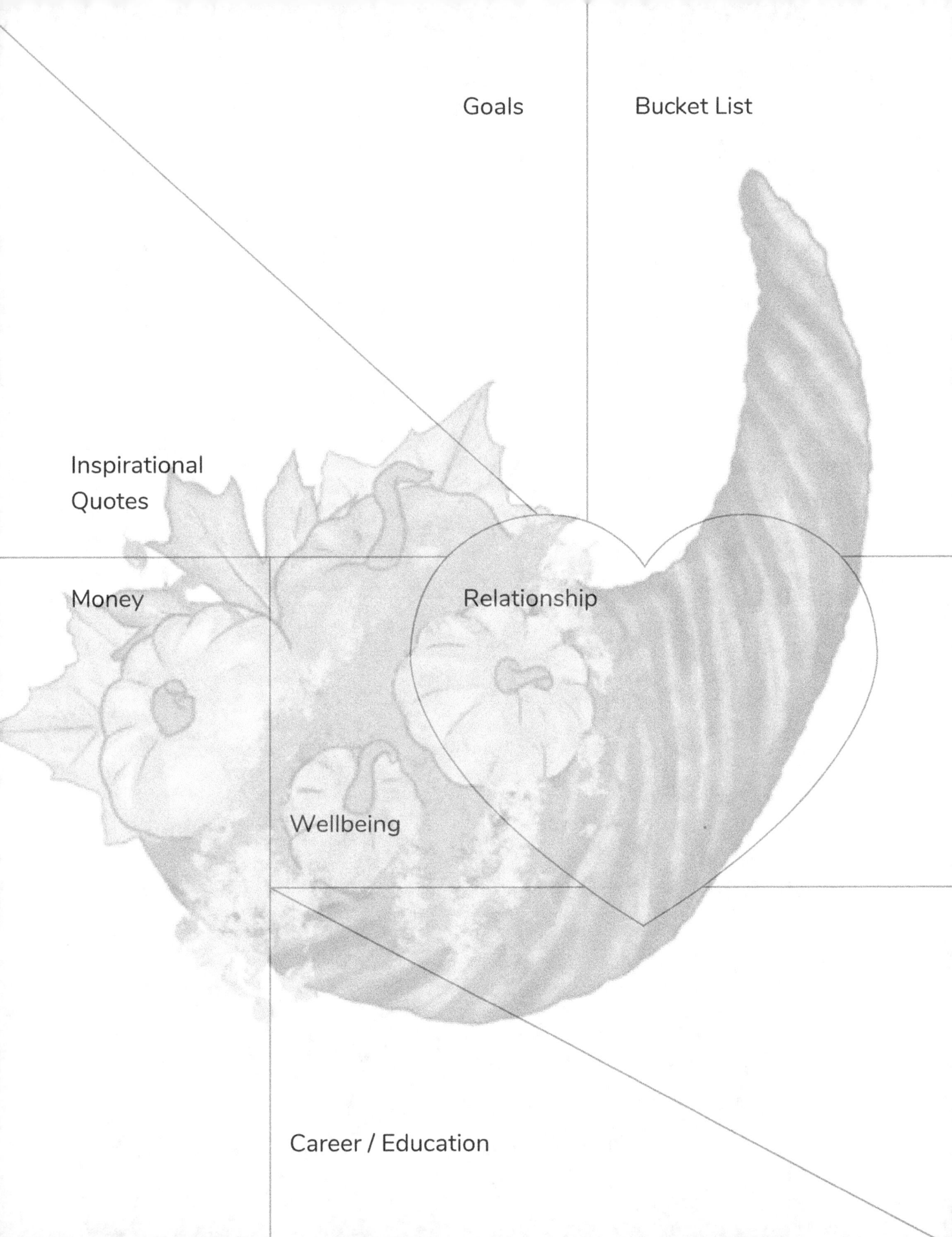

Goals

Bucket List

Inspirational Quotes

Money

Relationship

Wellbeing

Career / Education

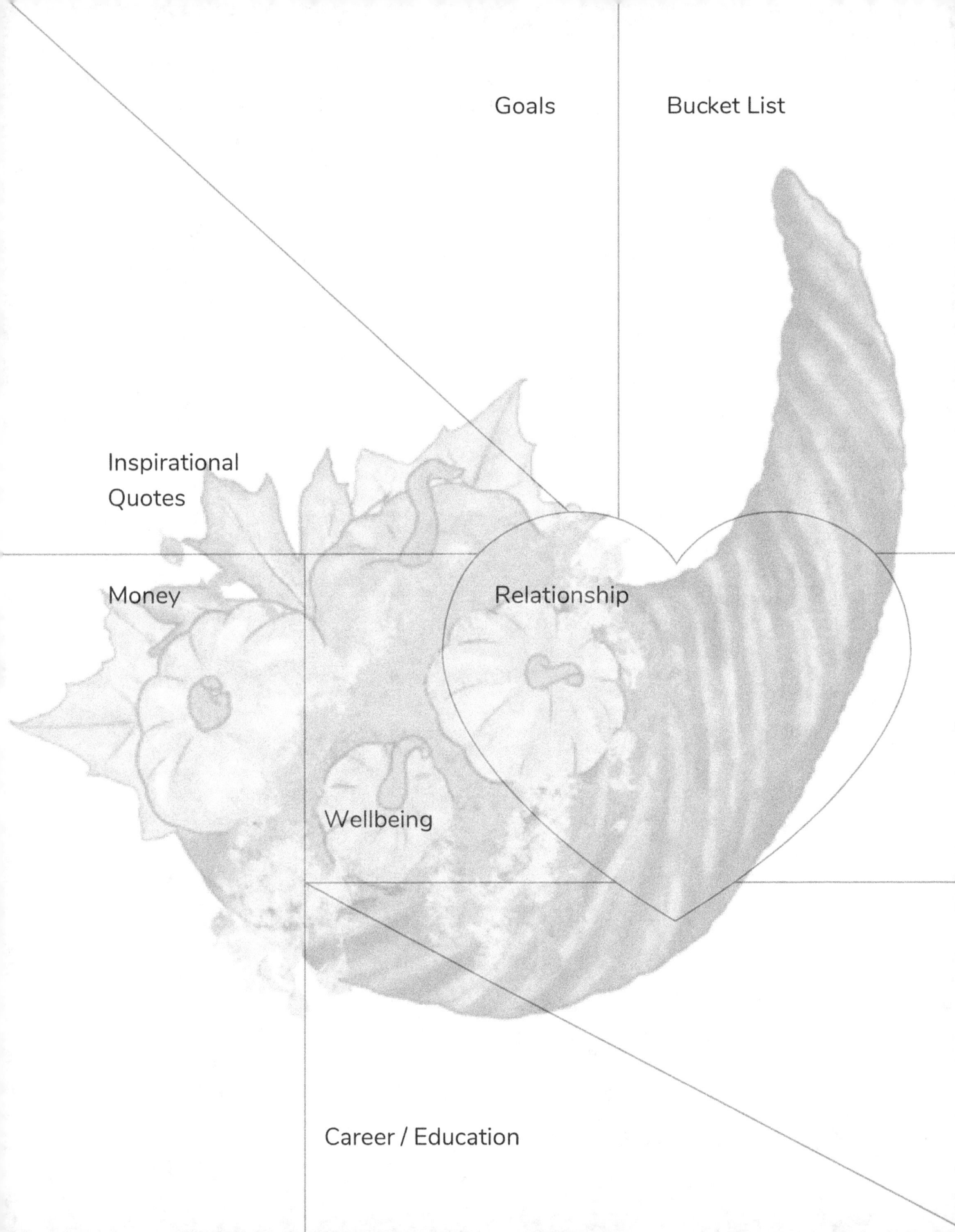

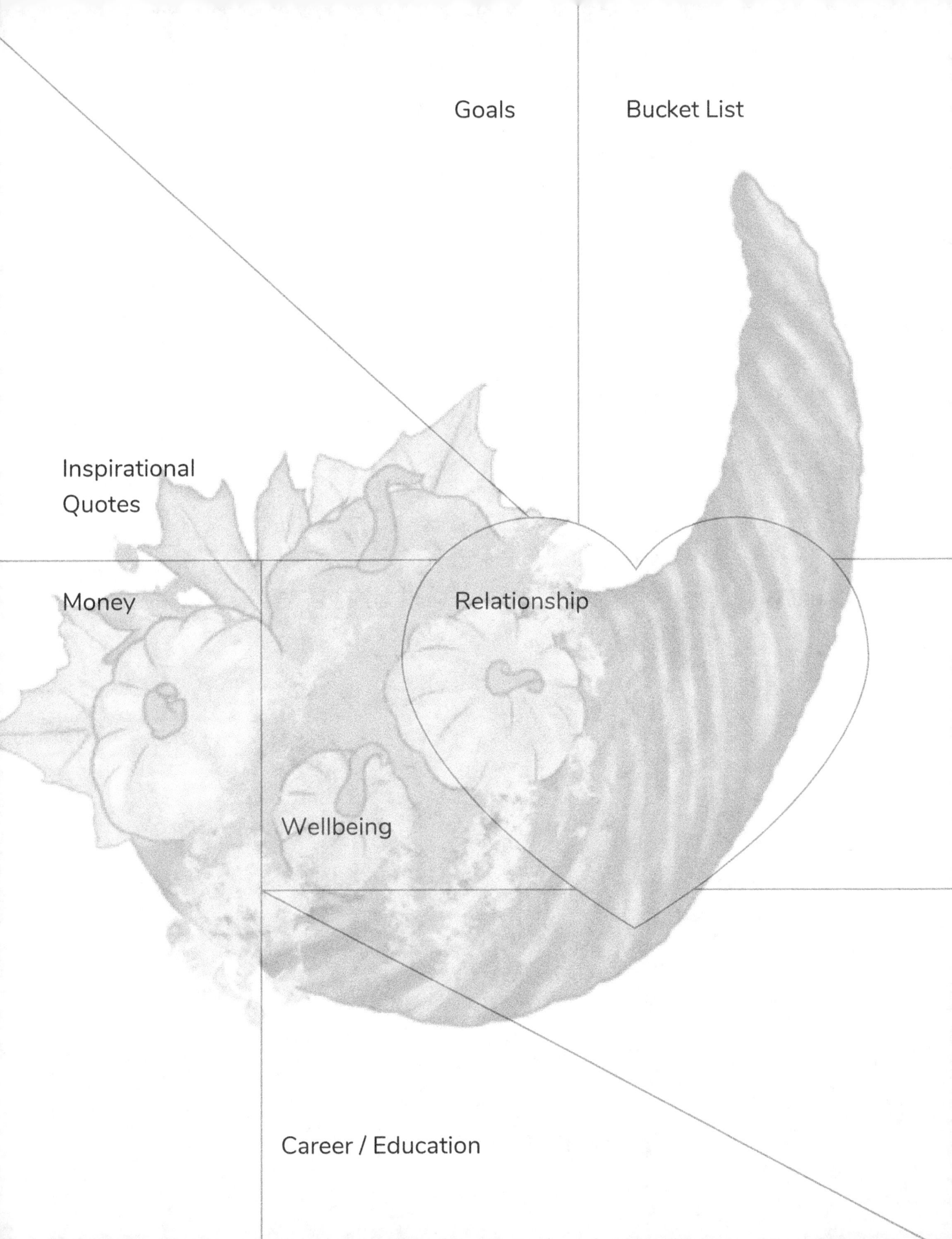

Goals

Bucket List

Inspirational Quotes

Money

Relationship

Wellbeing

Career / Education

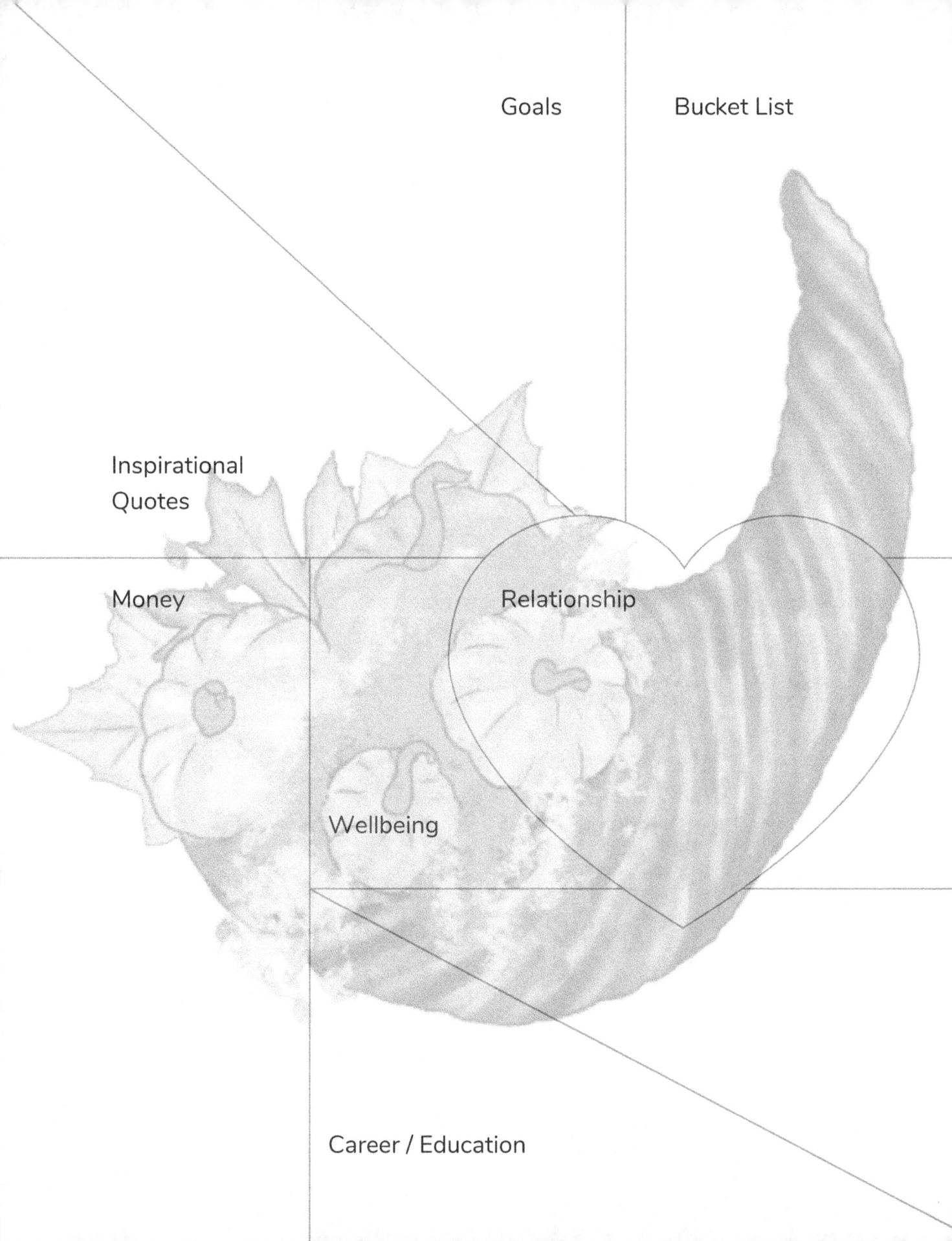

Goals

Bucket List

Inspirational Quotes

Money

Relationship

Wellbeing

Career / Education

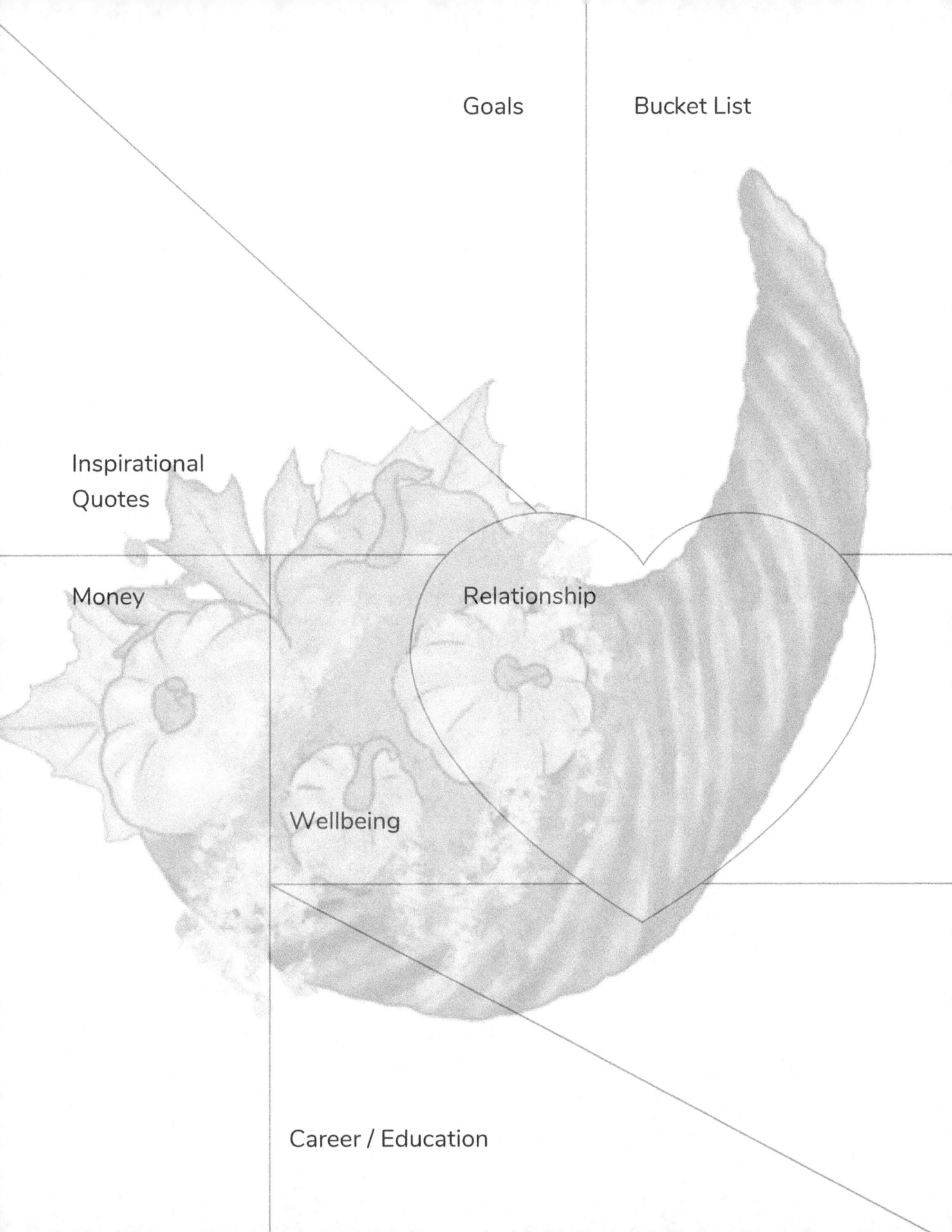

Goals Bucket List

Inspirational Quotes

Money

Relationship

Wellbeing

Career / Education

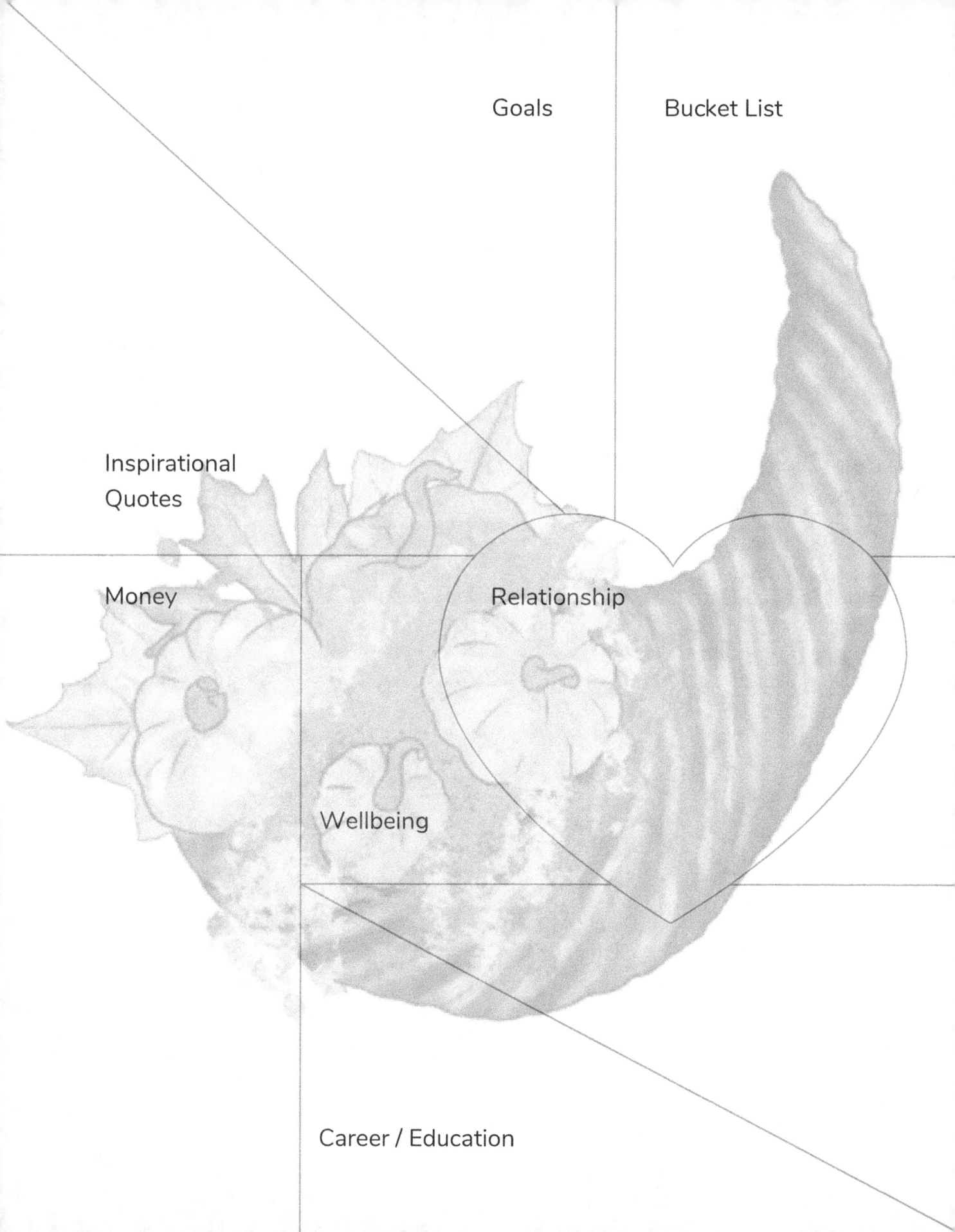

Goals

Bucket List

Inspirational Quotes

Money

Relationship

Wellbeing

Career / Education

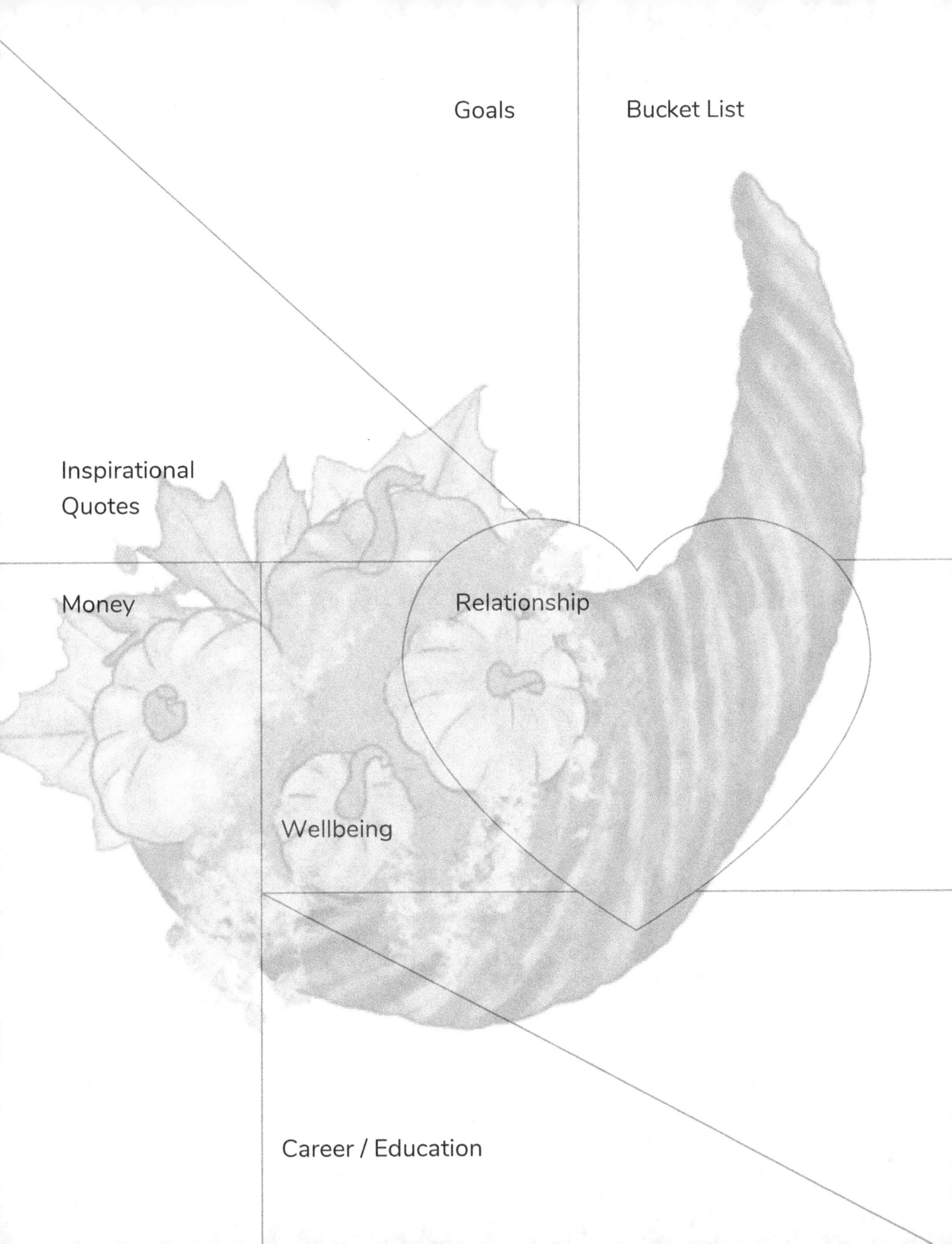

Goals Bucket List

Inspirational Quotes

Money

Relationship

Wellbeing

Career / Education

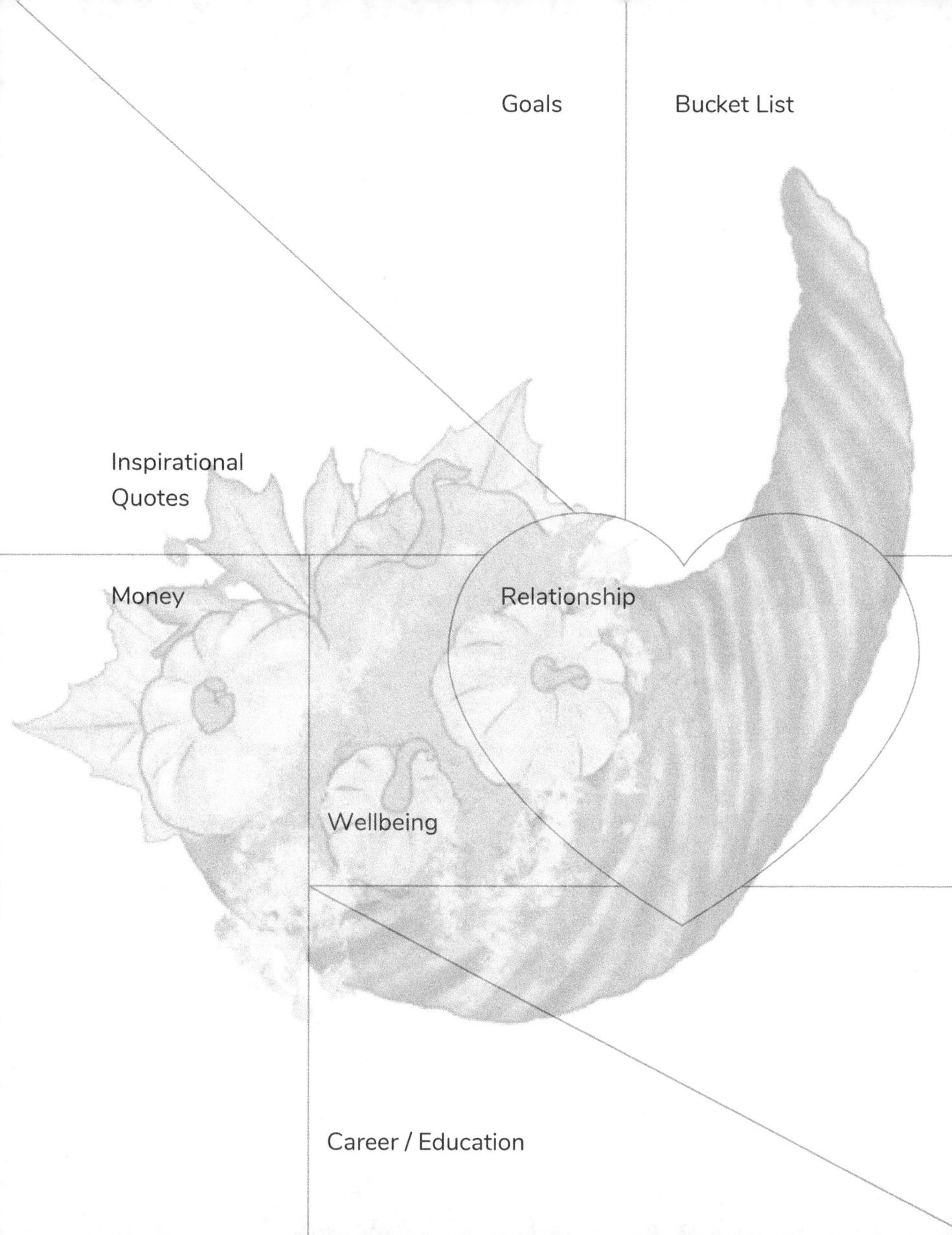

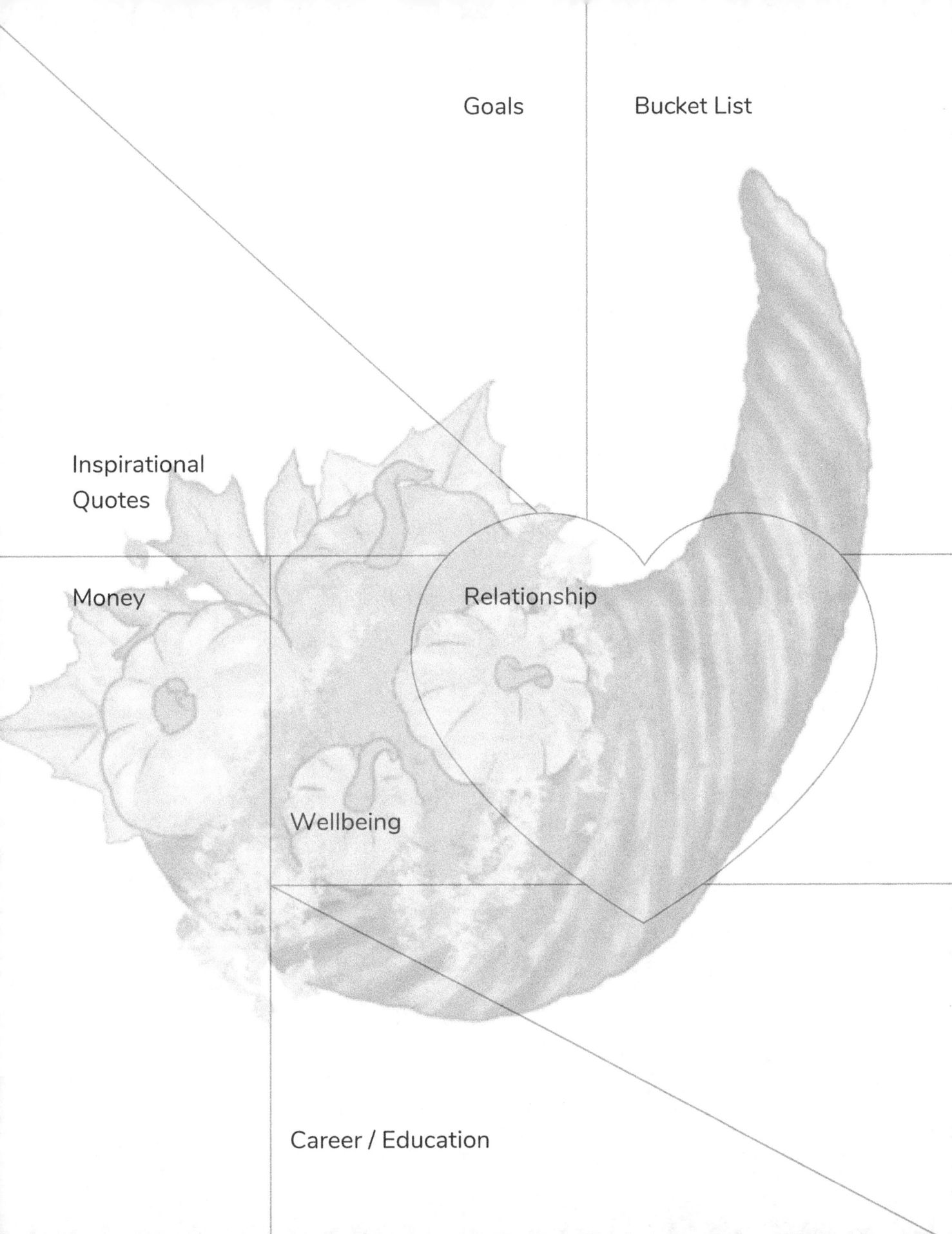

Goals

Bucket List

Inspirational Quotes

Money

Relationship

Wellbeing

Career / Education

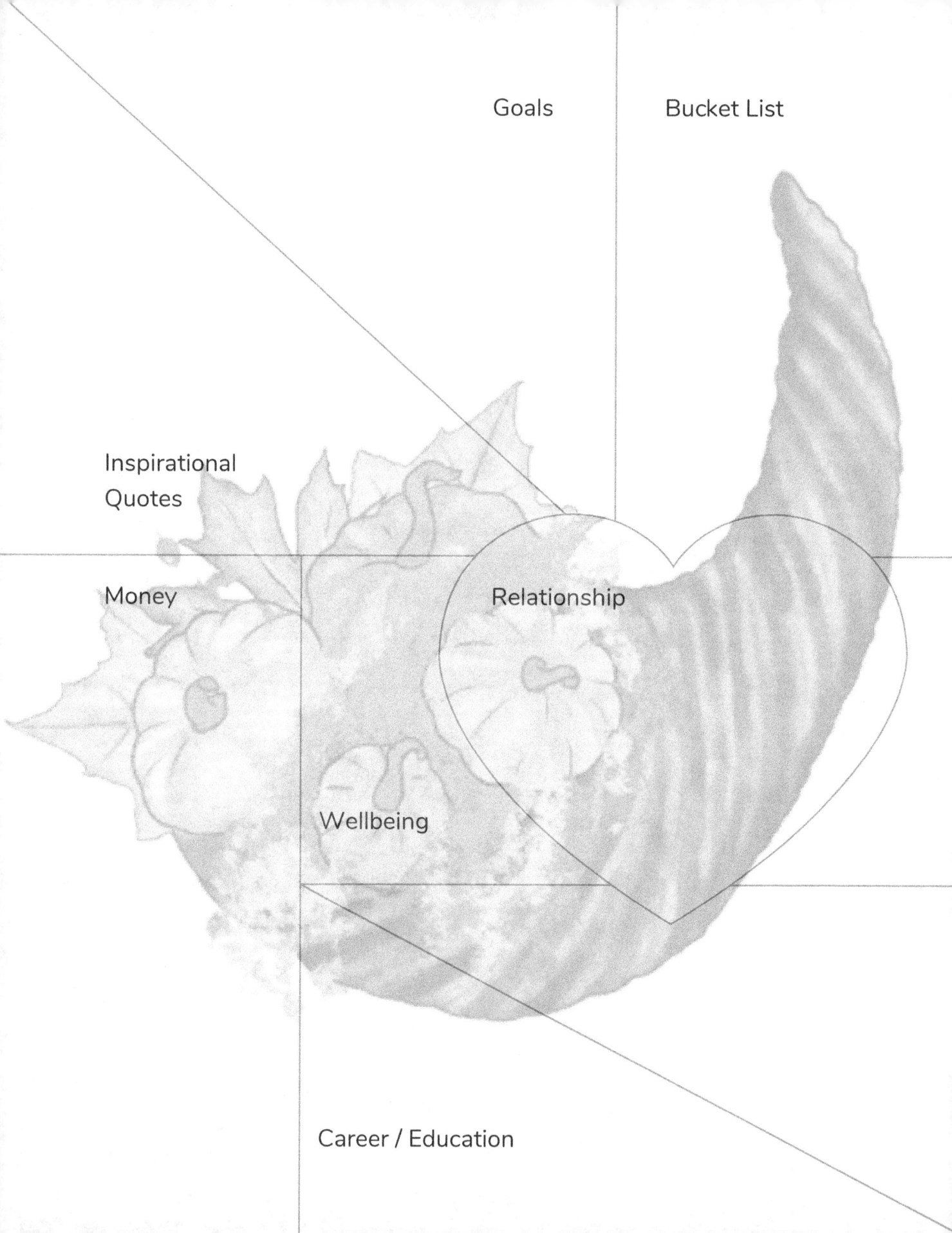

Goals

Bucket List

Inspirational Quotes

Money

Relationship

Wellbeing

Career / Education

November 2020

Sunday	Monday	Tuesday	Wednesday	Thursday	Friday	Saturday
1	2	3	4	5	6	7
8	9	10	11	12	13	14
15	16	17	18	19	20	21
22	23	24	25	26	27	28
29	30	1	2	3	4	5

_____

_____

_____

_____

December 2020

Sunday	Monday	Tuesday	Wednesday	Thursday	Friday	Saturday
29	30	1	2	3	4	5
6	7	8	9	10	11	12
13	14	15	16	17	18	19
20	21	22	23	24	25	26
27	28	29	30	31	1	2

_____

_____

_____

_____

Monthly Planner

Month: _____ **Year:** _____

Monday	Tuesday	Wednesday	Thursday	Friday	Saturday	Sunday
☐	☐	☐	☐	☐	☐	☐
☐	☐	☐	☐	☐	☐	☐
☐	☐	☐	☐	☐	☐	☐
☐	☐	☐	☐	☐	☐	☐
☐	☐	☐	☐	☐	☐	☐

Notes:

Monthly Planner

Month: _____   Year: _____

Monday	Tuesday	Wednesday	Thursday	Friday	Saturday	Sunday
☐	☐	☐	☐	☐	☐	☐
☐	☐	☐	☐	☐	☐	☐
☐	☐	☐	☐	☐	☐	☐
☐	☐	☐	☐	☐	☐	☐
☐	☐	☐	☐	☐	☐	☐

Notes:
_____
_____
_____
_____
_____
_____
_____
_____

Monthly Planner

Month: _____ Year: _____

Monday	Tuesday	Wednesday	Thursday	Friday	Saturday	Sunday
☐	☐	☐	☐	☐	☐	☐
☐	☐	☐	☐	☐	☐	☐
☐	☐	☐	☐	☐	☐	☐
☐	☐	☐	☐	☐	☐	☐
☐	☐	☐	☐	☐	☐	☐

Notes:
_____
_____
_____
_____
_____
_____
_____
_____
_____

Monthly Planner

Month: _____ **Year:** _____

Monday	Tuesday	Wednesday	Thursday	Friday	Saturday	Sunday
☐	☐	☐	☐	☐	☐	☐
☐	☐	☐	☐	☐	☐	☐
☐	☐	☐	☐	☐	☐	☐
☐	☐	☐	☐	☐	☐	☐
☐	☐	☐	☐	☐	☐	☐

Notes:
_____
_____
_____
_____
_____
_____
_____

Monthly Planner

Month: _____ Year: _____

Monday	Tuesday	Wednesday	Thursday	Friday	Saturday	Sunday
☐	☐	☐	☐	☐	☐	☐
☐	☐	☐	☐	☐	☐	☐
☐	☐	☐	☐	☐	☐	☐
☐	☐	☐	☐	☐	☐	☐
☐	☐	☐	☐	☐	☐	☐

Notes:
_____
_____
_____
_____
_____
_____
_____
_____
_____

Monthly Planner

Month: _____   Year: _____

Monday	Tuesday	Wednesday	Thursday	Friday	Saturday	Sunday
☐	☐	☐	☐	☐	☐	☐
☐	☐	☐	☐	☐	☐	☐
☐	☐	☐	☐	☐	☐	☐
☐	☐	☐	☐	☐	☐	☐
☐	☐	☐	☐	☐	☐	☐

Notes:
_____
_____
_____
_____
_____
_____
_____
_____

Monthly Planner

Month: _____ **Year:** _____

Monday	Tuesday	Wednesday	Thursday	Friday	Saturday	Sunday
☐	☐	☐	☐	☐	☐	☐
☐	☐	☐	☐	☐	☐	☐
☐	☐	☐	☐	☐	☐	☐
☐	☐	☐	☐	☐	☐	☐
☐	☐	☐	☐	☐	☐	☐

Notes:

Monthly Planner

Month: _____ **Year:** _____

Monday	Tuesday	Wednesday	Thursday	Friday	Saturday	Sunday
☐	☐	☐	☐	☐	☐	☐
☐	☐	☐	☐	☐	☐	☐
☐	☐	☐	☐	☐	☐	☐
☐	☐	☐	☐	☐	☐	☐
☐	☐	☐	☐	☐	☐	☐

Notes:
_____
_____
_____
_____
_____
_____
_____
_____

Monthly Planner

Month: _____ **Year:** _____

Monday	Tuesday	Wednesday	Thursday	Friday	Saturday	Sunday
☐	☐	☐	☐	☐	☐	☐
☐	☐	☐	☐	☐	☐	☐
☐	☐	☐	☐	☐	☐	☐
☐	☐	☐	☐	☐	☐	☐
☐	☐	☐	☐	☐	☐	☐

Notes:
_____
_____
_____
_____
_____
_____
_____
_____

Monthly Planner

Month: _____ Year: _____

Monday	Tuesday	Wednesday	Thursday	Friday	Saturday	Sunday
☐	☐	☐	☐	☐	☐	☐
☐	☐	☐	☐	☐	☐	☐
☐	☐	☐	☐	☐	☐	☐
☐	☐	☐	☐	☐	☐	☐
☐	☐	☐	☐	☐	☐	☐

Notes:
_____
_____
_____
_____
_____
_____
_____
_____

www.ingramcontent.com/pod-product-compliance
Lightning Source LLC
LaVergne TN
LVHW060135080526
838202LV00050B/4124